Quincy
Question Mark

Written by Barbara Cooper
Illustrated by Maggie Raynor

GARETH**STEVENS**
GS PUBLISHING
A World Almanac Education Group Company

Please visit our web site at: www.garethstevens.com
For a free color catalog describing Gareth Stevens Publishing's
list of high-quality books and multimedia programs, call
1-800-542-2595 (USA) or 1-800-387-3178 (Canada).
Gareth Stevens Publishing's fax: (414) 332-3567.

Library of Congress Cataloging-in-Publication Data

Cooper, Barbara, 1929-
    [Quentin Question Mark]
    Quincy Question Mark / written by Barbara Cooper; illustrated by Maggie
Raynor. — North American ed.
        p. cm. — (Meet the Puncs: A remarkable punctuation family)
    Summary: Introduces the use of the question mark through the story of Quincy,
a member of the Punc family who has always been extremely nosy.
    ISBN 0-8368-4228-6 (lib. bdg.)
    [1. English language—Interrogative—Fiction. 2. English language—Punctuation—
Fiction.] I. Raynor, Maggie, 1946- , ill. II. Title.
PZ7.C78467Qu   2004
[E]—dc22   2004045320

This edition first published in 2005 by
Gareth Stevens Publishing
A World Almanac Education Group Company
330 West Olive Street, Suite 100
Milwaukee, Wisconsin 53212 USA

This U.S. edition copyright © 2005 by Gareth Stevens, Inc. Original edition
copyright © 2003 by Compass Books Ltd., UK. First published in 2003 as
(The Puncs) an adventure in punctuation: Quentin Question Mark by Compass
Books Ltd.

Designed and produced by Allegra Publishing Ltd., London
Gareth Stevens editor: Dorothy L. Gibbs
Gareth Stevens art direction: Tammy West

Printed in the United States of America

1 2 3 4 5 6 7 8 9 08 07 06 05 04

Have you ever heard of **Quincy Question Mark?**

He is the nosiest of the Puncs. He never stops asking questions, which is why he is good at his job. Quincy is an airport security officer.

3

Would you be surprised to learn that Quincy has been nosy since the day he was born?

Can you guess what his very first words were?

Are you wondering who Quincy's parents are?

Do you have a moment?

His mother, Wynonna, works for the P. A. P. "What is that?" you may ask. P. A. P. stands for Punc Advertising Polls.

Wynonna stops people in the streets and asks them questions.

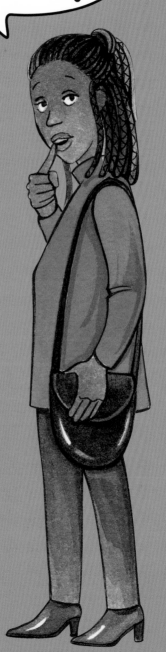

May I think about it?

"How often do you eat chocolate cookies?"

"What kind of toothpaste do you use?"

What about Quincy's father? His name is Wyatt. He works for a magazine called *Punc Life*. What does he do there? He writes quizzes that ask tricky questions.

"Who was the first Punc to fly over the Alps in a hang glider?"

Punc Life

Have you guessed that Wyatt goes
hang gliding on weekends?

All through his childhood,
Quincy wore out his parents
with his endless questions.
He didn't give them
a moment's peace.

Wyatt and
Wynonna could
not even watch
their favorite
TV shows.

"What have we done to deserve this?" they would ask each other as Quincy jumped up and down on the sofa, shouting,

"Who's that?"

"What is he doing?"

"Where is he going?"

Every morning, as Quincy was leaving for school, Wynonna would stand at the front door with a list of questions.

"Did you wash your hands?"

"Have you brushed your teeth?"

"Do you have your lunch money?"

And what do you think happened at school? That's right! Quincy drove everyone crazy with his questions.

"How did King Puncsutawney break his neck?"

"Where does Space end?"

Whenever Quincy raised his hand in class, all the other students would groan, and his teacher would mumble "oh no" under her breath.

Have you noticed that Quincy is rather pale? Would you like to know why?

He's pale because he doesn't spend any time outdoors. Quincy likes to sit indoors. When he's not working at the airport, he spends most of his time working with his stamp collection.

What do you think about that?

"Where on Earth
is Alapalapunc?"

Can you see how being an airport security officer suits Quincy**?** At the airport, he spends all day indoors, asking passengers all kinds of questions.

"Have you read this notice, Madam**?**"

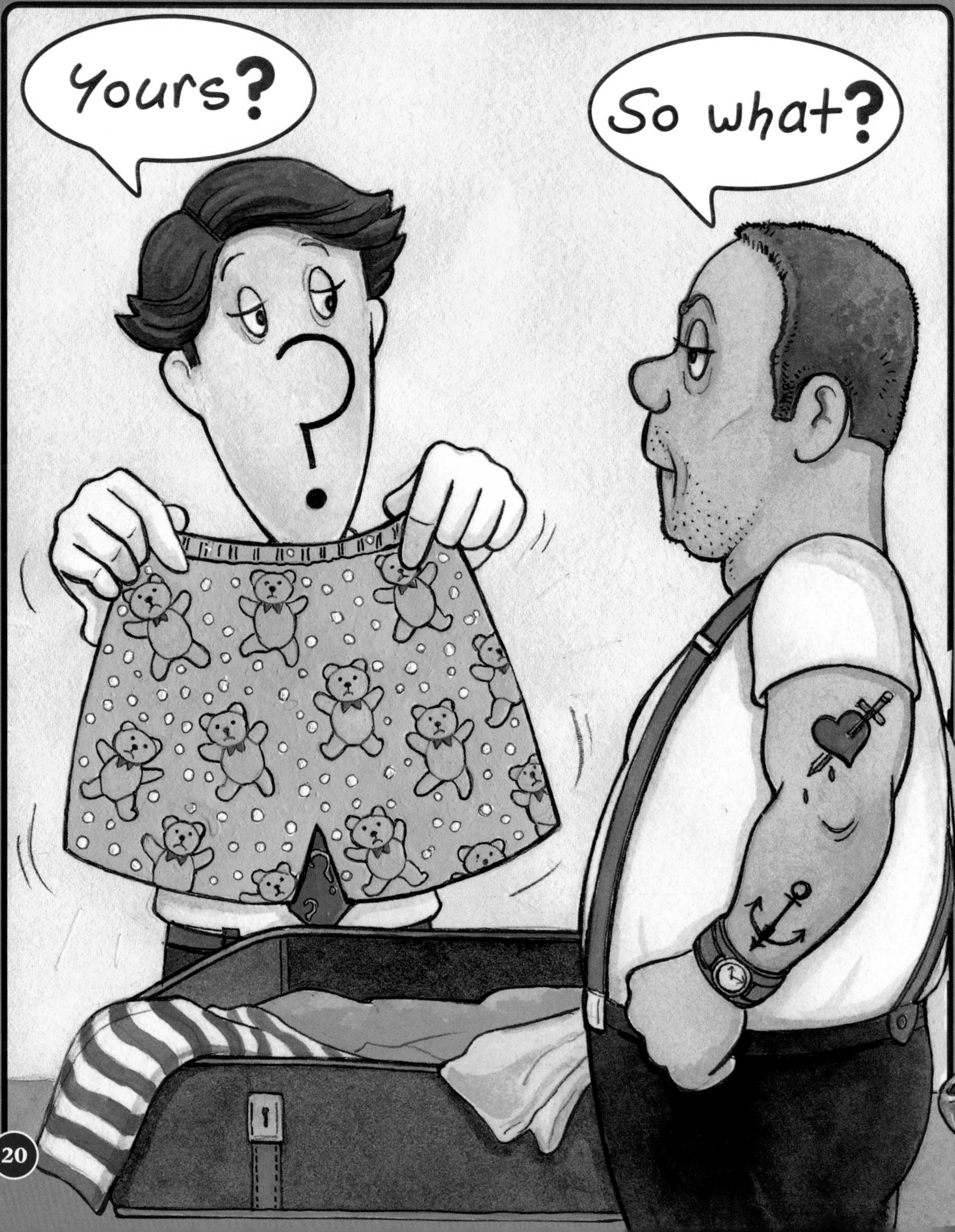
Yours?
So what?

Quincy often makes passengers open their baggage.

"What have you got in here?" he asks.

Sometimes, he picks things up (which is why he wears white gloves), asking

"Where did you buy this?"

"How much did you pay for it?"

Would you believe there was a time when Quincy didn't speak at all?

Can you guess why?

Do you think it might have been the time he found a snake in someone's luggage?

23

Would you like to know if Quincy has a wife?

Why, yes, he has. Her name is Wykini (Kini for short).

Do you want to know where Kini's unusual name came from?

She was named after her great-great-great grandmother, Waquini, who was a Native American from Wyoming.

Can you guess what Kini's job is? She works in a customer service department, where she spends most of the day asking people questions and filling out forms.

"What is your home address?"

"When is your date of birth?"

"Do you have a cell phone or fax number?"

"How will you pay your bill?"

Quincy and Kini have a very happy marriage. Do you know why?

It is because they just ask each other questions and don't care about answers.

Kini: "How was your day?"

Quincy: "What's for supper?"

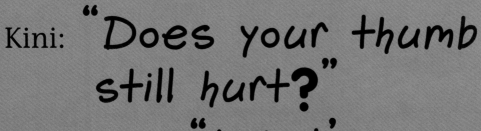

Kini: "Does your thumb still hurt?"

Quincy: "What's wrong with the TV?"

Do you know anyone quite like Quincy and Kini?

What word would you use to describe Quincy?

Did you say "inquisitive"**?**

Did you say "inquiring"**?**

Did you say "curious"**?**

Did you say "nosy"**?**

Whatever you say, you can be sure that wherever and whenever and however there are questions to be asked — whoever asks them — you will find Quincy, won't you**?**

Quincy's Checklist

- **Use a question mark, instead of a period, at the end of a sentence that asks a question:**
  Have you ever heard of Quincy Question Mark?

- **Any asking-word can be followed by a question mark:**
  Who? What? When? Where? Why? How?

- **Use a question mark even when a sentence is half statement and half question:**
  You will find Quincy anywhere there is a question, won't you?

- **You might find a question mark in parentheses to show that there is doubt about the word or statement after which the question mark appears:**
  The first issue of *Punc Life* magazine was published in 1901(?).

- **Quiz books are full of questions (and question marks) that test your knowledge:**
  How did King Puncsutawney break his neck?

- **Teachers ask difficult questions:**
  How do you spell "Alapalapunc"?

- **Doctors ask personal questions:**
  How old are you?
  How much do you weigh?

- **People often ask questions when they argue:**
  Why should I?
  What do you mean?
  How could you?

- **In cartoons, comic strips, and advertisements, you might see a row of question marks, just for fun or, perhaps, to make the question stand out:**
  W-w-what's happening?????

- **For impact, a question mark might be placed next to an exclamation point:**
  Are you crazy?!

- **Remember:** Asking questions is good. It means that you are curious and like to learn about things. Silly questions or asking too many questions, however, can be very annoying, especially if you don't even bother listening to the answers.